MY FIRST
GARDEN
B·O·O·K

ANGELA WILKES

DORLING KINDERSLEY
London • New York • Stuttgart

A Dorling Kindersley Book

For Rose

Design Mathewson Bull
Photography Dave King
Editor Helen Drew
Production Marguerite Fenn

Managing Editor Jane Yorke
Art Director Roger Priddy

First published in Great Britain in 1992 by
Dorling Kindersley Limited, London
9 Henrietta Street, London WC2E 8PS

**A CIP catalogue record for this book
is available from the British Library**

ISBN 0-86318-740-4

Phototypeset by Setting Studio, Newcastle
Colour reproduction by Colourscan, Singapore
Printed and bound in Italy by L.E.G.O.

Dorling Kinderley would like to thank Jonathan Buckley,
Mandy Earey, Richard Gilbert and June King for their help
in producing this book.

Illustrations by Brian Delf

CONTENTS

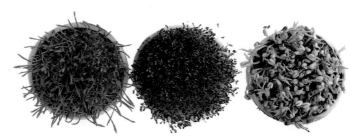

GARDENING BY PICTURES

Growing things is easy and fun and you do not need a garden! **My First Garden Book** shows you how to grow flowers, herbs, fruit and vegetables on window-sills, balconies and patios. Step-by-step photographs show you exactly what to do and there are life-size photographs of the finished projects. On the opposite page is a list of things to read before you start and below are the points to look for in each project.

How to use this book

The things you need
The plants and things you need for each project are shown life-size, to help you check you have everything.

Gardener's tools
These illustrated checklists show you which pieces of equipment to have ready before you start a project.

Step-by-step
Step-by-step photographs and clear instructions show you what to do at each stage of the project.

WINDOW GARDEN

With a window box you can look out on to a mass of flowers without having to go outside. Choose flowers in one or two colours, or go for a riot of bright colours. Look out for plants with interesting leaves, and for trailing plants to go at the front of the window box. Here you can see what to do. The final result is over the page.

GARDENER'S TOOLS

Trowel
Scissors
Plant food
Water spray
Watering can

You will need

Small plants (two or three of each sort)

Marguerite

Soil-based potting compost

Clay pellets, gravel or crocks

A window box with drainage holes in the bottom

Bellflower

Busy Lizzy

Pansy

Drip tray

40

What to do

1 Fill the bottom of the window box with a layer of clay pellets about 3 cm deep, to stop the compost going soggy.

2 Half fill the window box with potting compost. If the compost is very dry, water it before you start planting anything.

3 Keeping the plants in their pots, arrange where to put them. Tall plants should go at the back and trailing ones at the front.

4 One at a time, take each plant out of its pot and gently loosen its roots, by pulling them free from potting compost.

5 Dig a small hole. Gently put the first plant in, making sure its roots have enough room. Press down the compost round the plant.

6 Plant the other plants. Fill in the gaps between them with compost and press it down firmly, leaving space for watering.

41

Things to remember

1. Read the instructions before you start, to make sure you have everything you need.

2. Check when to plant different things and which growing conditions they like best.

3. Put on an apron or old shirt and roll up your sleeves before you start.

4. Cover your worktable with newspaper before you start each project.

5. When you have finished planting things, clean your garden tools, tidy up any mess, and put everything away.

6. Water and check your seeds, pips, and plants regularly once you have planted them and watch them as they grow.

7. Be patient. Do not give up if things do not start to grow straightaway.

The final results
Life-size pictures show you what the finished projects look like, making it easy for you to copy them.

Aftercare
Many of the projects have step-by-step instructions showing you how to care for the things you have planted.

Information
The finished projects often have notes around them, telling you more about particular plants.

GARDEN IN BLOOM

And here is the finished window box! You can copy this one, or try your own plant arrangements. Ask an adult to help you move the full window box as it is heavy and must sit safely on a strong window ledge. If the window ledge slopes a little, wedge pieces of wood under the front of the box, to keep it level.

Watering
Water the window box enough to keep the compost slightly moist. It will need watering every day in warm weather.

Dead-heading
The plants in the window box will flower for longer if you regularly pick or snip off any dead flower heads.

Feeding
Once every six weeks or so, "feed" the plants by adding a little liquid plant food to the water in your watering can.

Pest control
The simplest way to get rid of greenfly on the plants is to spray them with warm water with washing-up liquid added to it.

New plants
If one of the plants in the window box dies, carefully dig it up. Plant another plant in its place, pressing the compost firmly around it.

The finished window box

MARGUERITE
This is a small bushy plant that produces pretty daisy-like flowers throughout the summer.

BUSY LIZZY (Impatiens)
Easy to look after, these plants have flat-faced, brightly coloured flowers. They will stay in flower for most of the summer.

PANSY
We used two apricot-coloured pansies and two purple ones. Keep pansies well-watered and dead-head them often.

BELLFLOWER (Campanula)
This trailing variety of bellflower can also be grown as an indoor plant. It blooms from late summer to early winter.

42

43

GARDEN KIT

Here are some of the tools and other things that you will need to start gardening. They are usually shown in the Gardener's tools boxes in the book. Gather the things for your kit together and you will be ready to start planting and watching things grow!

Potting compost. This is light soil with plant food added to it. There are different types of potting compost: some for seeds and cuttings and others for larger plants

Gravel (or clay pellets), to stop the holes in flowerpots getting blocked

Small watering can

Liquid plant food, to replace the minerals in compost that plants use up

Scissors

Seed trays with drainage holes in the bottom

Drip trays to match the different sizes of your flowerpots

Water spray

6

Marker pen, for labelling things

Teaspoon, for moving seedlings

Trowel

Small fork

Garden twine or string

Garden sticks, for supporting droopy plants

Flowerpots in different sizes with drainage holes in the bottom

Small envelopes, for collecting seeds

Ties, for holding plants to sticks

Plant labels

Polythene bags, for covering flowerpots when planting seeds

SEED SEARCH

You can easily buy flower seeds, but it is far more interesting to collect them yourself. Seeds come in a fascinating variety of shapes and sizes, depending on how different plants scatter them. You can gather flower seeds throughout the summer and tree seeds in the autumn. Here are some of the more interesting types of seed that you may find.

Collecting seeds

Look for seeds once a flower's petals have died and a seed head has formed. The seeds are ripe when they are brown. Cut off the seed head and shake the seeds into a paper bag. Put the seeds in a small envelope, seal and label it, and keep it in a cool, dark place.

HONESTY

Honesty has flat, round seed pods that turn silver when the seeds are ripe. Rub the pods between your fingers to release the seeds.

POPPY

Poppies have seed pods like pepper pots. When the wind blows, the fine seeds are shaken out of the seed heads.

SWEET PEA

Collect the seed pods when they are turning brown. Snap them open to find the seeds.

NIGELLA

This flower has puffed-up seed pods. The seeds are ripe when the pods turn brown.

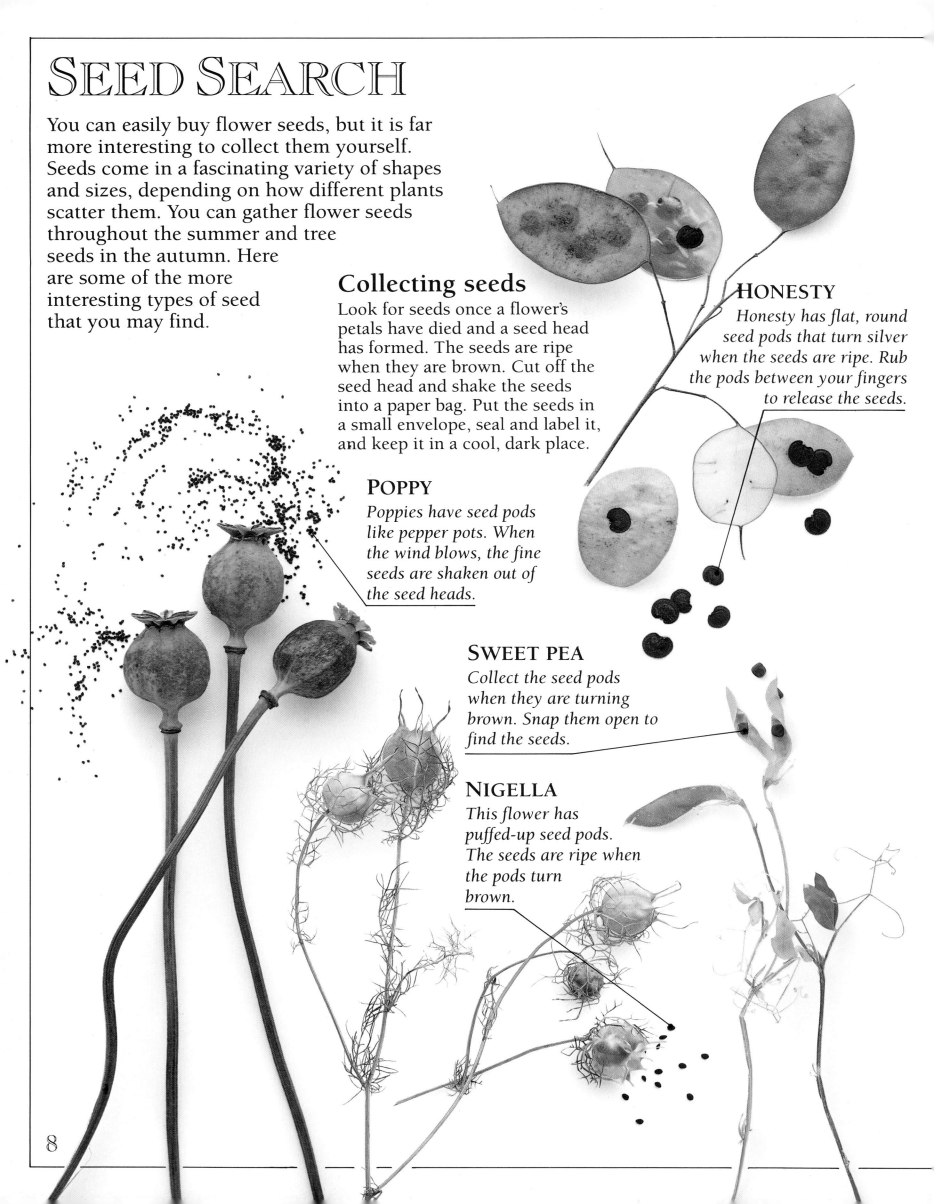

Tree seeds

It is best to look for tree seeds early in the autumn, before the birds and animals have removed them. Store tree seeds in a cool, dark place until the end of the winter, then plant them.

PLANE TREE
The seeds are encased in unusual "bobbles".

SYCAMORE
Each set of "wings" carries two seeds.

ACORNS
These are the seeds of the oak tree.

HORSE CHESTNUTS
The shiny seeds are carried in prickly cases.

SUNFLOWER
The striped seeds are packed together in unusual patterns on the massive flowerheads.

HOLLYHOCK
Pick the seed heads from the tall stems once the flowers have died.

MARIGOLD
Marigolds have tight clusters of crescent-shaped seeds which turn brown as they ripen.

PLANTING SEEDS

If you plant flower seeds indoors in early spring they will be big enough to plant outside once the weather is warmer. You can grow most *annuals* and *biennials** from seed. Read the backs of seed packets to find out exactly when to plant different flowers, which growing conditions they need, and how often to water them.

You will need

*Seed and cutting compost***

Acorns

Ties for plastic bags

Nasturtium seeds

Plant labels

Sunflower seeds

Poppy seeds

Plastic bags

What to do

GARDENER'S TOOLS

Seed trays

Flowerpots and drip trays

Trowel

Watering can with rose

Pen (for labels)

1 Fill the flowerpots and seed trays with compost to about 1 cm down from the top of the pot. Water the compost lightly.

2 Planting big seeds. Push each one about 1 cm deep into the compost. Label each pot with the name of the seed you have planted.

10

* Annuals live for one year. Biennials live for two years, but usually only flower the second year.

** Special compost for young plants.

From seed to plant

Some of the easiest flowers to grow are nasturtiums. Here you can see how a seedling develops. This plant stayed in one pot, but seedlings planted in seed trays will need to be carefully dug up and moved to separate pots, or into the garden, once they are big enough.

1

You can just see the nasturtium's first two leaves.

3 Plant small seeds in seed trays. Sprinkle the seeds on to the compost. Cover them with a thin layer of compost. Label the tray.

2

The seedling grows fast. The first two leaves grow bigger. The stem shoots up between them and more leaves appear. The young plant needs a lot of light.

4 Tie plastic bags over the flowerpots and seed trays and put them in a warm, dark place†. Check the seeds every day.

3

4

5 As soon as shoots appear, take off the plastic bags and move the seeds into the light. Water the compost enough to keep it damp.

†Such as an airing cupboard.

Buds appear, then the nasturtium starts to flower. As it is a climbing plant, you should tie it to a garden stick as it grows bigger. The plant will twine round the stick.

11

SALAD GARDEN

You don't always need flowerpots and potting compost to grow things. You can grow all sorts of tasty, crunchy things to add to salads on nothing more than cotton wool soaked in water. Try sprouting different seeds, beans and grains and you can harvest your own mini-crops of vitamin-packed salad sprouts in about a week. The seeds will sprout all the year round and you can grow them on a window-sill or in any light place indoors. The best place to buy the things you need is a health food shop.

You will need

Different seeds:

Wheat grains

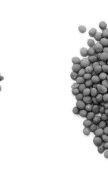

Alfalfa seeds   *Mustard seeds*

Mung beans

Cress seeds

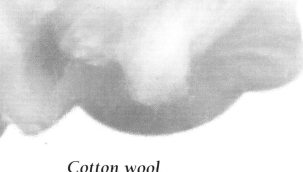
Cotton wool

GARDENER'S TOOLS

Shallow dishes *Ties* *Plastic bags* *Bowl* *Sieve* *Jam jars* *Pen* *Labels* *Water spray*

What to do

1 Rinse large beans and grains in a sieve under a cold tap. Put each sort in a jar of warm water to soak for 12 hours, then rinse them.

2 Dip pieces of cotton wool in cold water, then gently squeeze most of the water out. Line the dishes with the damp cotton wool.

3 Sprinkle a tablespoonful of one type of bean or grain over the cotton wool in each bowl. Label each one to say what is in it.

4 Tie plastic bags loosely over the bowls, to keep the seeds moist. Put the bowls in a warm, dark place. Check them every day.

5 As soon as the seeds sprout, take off the plastic bags and move them to a light place. Spray them with water every day.

The sprouting seeds

Most of the seeds, beans and grains will have started to sprout in two to three days. They will be ready to pick after five to seven days, when they are still young and tender. Snip them off the cotton wool and sprinkle them on salads or add them to sandwiches.

MUNG BEANS

These are the classic Chinese bean sprouts. Pick them when they are still pale and have no leaves.

ALFALFA

This grows very quickly and looks like cress with smaller leaves.

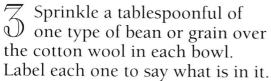

WHEAT

This looks like young grass. Snip it and sprinkle it on salads or add it to your pet's food.

BULBS

Many of the prettiest spring flowers grow from bulbs and are easy to grow indoors. Buy bulbs in autumn and plant them straightaway, to flower the next spring. Choose small varieties to grow in small pots and grow only the same plants in any one pot, so that they all flower at the same time.

To bloom well, all bulbs have to be put in a cool, dark place for a while, to form strong roots. Turn the page to see a stunning array of flowers grown from bulbs.

You will need

Different bulbs:

Gravel or clay pellets

Hyacinths

Dwarf tulips

Daffodils

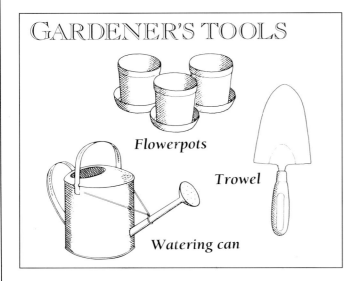

GARDENER'S TOOLS

Flowerpots

Trowel

Watering can

Planting bulbs

1 Shovel a little gravel or some clay pellets into the bottom of your flowerpots or containers, to stop the compost going soggy.

2 Half fill the flowerpots with potting compost. Instead of the potting compost you could use special bulb fibre if you like.

3 Arrange big bulbs close together with their pointed ends up. Add more compost. Let the bulbs poke out of the compost.

14

Potting compost

What is a bulb?

Here the bulb of a hyacinth in flower has been cut in half, so that you can see what is inside it.

Narcissi

Grape hyacinths

Crocuses

Miniature irises

Food supply

A bulb is like an onion inside. It is a kind of underground food store. The plant rests for most of the year, then uses the food in the bulb to grow.

Roots

Bulbs have to grow strong roots before they can be brought into the light.

4 Arrange small bulbs with the pointed ends up. Add enough compost to cover them and fill the pot to about 2 cm below the rim.

5 Water the pots, then put them in a cool, dark place for 8 to 12 weeks. Check the compost now and then, to make sure it is moist.

Turn the page to see what to do next.

SPRING FLOWERS

When the bulbs have shoots about 2 cm tall, move the flowerpots into the light, but keep them in a cool place. Most bulbs will flower four to five months after planting. They will flower best in a cool room. When the flowers have died, cut off the dead flower heads and let the leaves dry up, then plant the bulbs outside if you can, as they will not flower indoors again. The beautifully coloured flowers shown here all bloom in early spring.

CROCUS

*One of the first spring flowers, it has funnel-shaped white, purple, or yellow flowers. Grows from a corm.**

SCILLA

This tiny plant has small, bright blue, bell-shaped flowers.

DWARF DAFFODIL

"Tête-à-tête" is a tiny golden daffodil with swept-back petals. It is a member of the narcissus family of bulbs.

CHIONODOXA

Commonly known as "Glory-of-the-snow". Has starry blue flowers with white eyes.

A stem that grows under the surface of the soil.

PUSCHKINIA

This tiny rock garden plant has spikes of star-shaped white or pale blue flowers.

HYACINTH

Hyacinths have heavy spikes of sweetly scented flowers, which may need supporting with garden sticks. Try growing hyacinths in water in special bulb jars, so that you can watch the roots grow.

WATERLILY TULIP

A dwarf tulip which has white flowers with red and yellow centres. Like other lily-flowered tulips, the flowers open out flat in the sun.

HANGING BASKETS

A hanging basket is one of the prettiest mini-gardens you can make and you can hang it where you like. We used spring flowers in blues and yellows for our basket. For a summer basket, look for fuchsias, geraniums, busy Lizzies, and lobelia. Turn the page for the finished basket.

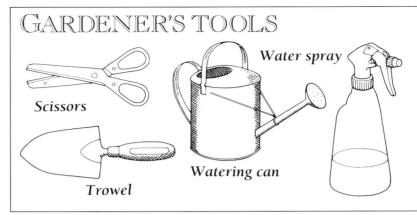

GARDENER'S TOOLS

Scissors

Trowel

Water spray

Watering can

You will need

Lightweight potting compost

Pansies

A wire basket with a chain handle

Grape hyacinths

Sphagnum moss

Plastic bin liner

Primulas or polyanthus

Drumstick primula

Trailing variegated ivy plants

Planting up the basket

1 Line the inside of the wire basket with a thickish layer of sphagnum moss. You should not be able to see any light through it.

2 Cut a piece of bin liner big enough to line the inside of the basket. Lay it over the moss and trim off any edges that show.

3 Wrap each ivy plant in a small piece of plastic shaped into a cone. The narrow end of the cone should be around the leaves.

19

GARDEN IN A BASKET

Here is the finished basket, overflowing with spring flowers. A hanging basket is very heavy when full, so ask an adult to hang it up for you and check that it is fastened securely. Hang it in a place where you can see the plants properly and make sure that it is low enough for you to water easily.

GRAPE HYACINTHS
These pretty spring flowers grow from bulbs, but you can buy them as plants too.

Planting up the basket (continued)

4 Make holes in the plastic liner. Thread the cone-wrapped leaves of the ivy plants through the holes. Pull the plastic cones away.

5 Thread a few more plants through the base of the basket in the same way, then half fill the basket with potting compost.

SPHAGNUM MOSS

CHAIN

PRIMULA

DRUMSTICK PRIMULA

There are many different sorts of primula. They all flower in early to mid spring.

PANSIES

These are winter-flowering pansies. They will flower throughout the winter and spring, as long as you dead-head them regularly.

VARIEGATED IVY

Trailing ivy plants are useful for hanging baskets as they provide greenery and trail prettily around the bottom of the basket.

6 Arrange and plant the rest of the plants in the basket. Fill the gaps between the plants with compost and water them well.

Watering

Water and spray the basket just enough to keep the compost damp. Baskets need watering once or twice a day in hot weather.

Dead–heading

The plants in the basket will last longer if you regularly snip off any dead flower heads or leaves. Replace any plants that die.

21

DESERT GARDEN

Buy some small succulents and you can create a miniature desert in your own home. Succulents are plants that can survive without much water as they store it in their fleshy leaves or stems. Choose non-prickly plants with contrasting shapes, colours and textures and try out different arrangements in a shallow container or tray. Turn the page to see a finished desert garden.

You will need
Small succulents:

Sedum sieboldii

GARDENER'S TOOLS

Small spoon

Trowel

Scissors

Watering can

Wart plant (Haworthia attenuata)

Gravel or coarse pebbles

Soil-based potting compost

Grit or coarse sand

Shallow container or deep tray

What to do

Hen and chickens (Echeveria)

Flaming Katy (Kalanchoe blossfeldiana)

Sedum*

1 Put a thin layer of gravel in the bottom of the container. Cover with potting compost until the container is half full.

2 Keeping the plants in their pots, try out different arrangements to see where you want to plant them.

3 Carefully remove the plants from their pots, one at a time, and plant them. Fill in the gaps between them with more compost.

4 Gently spoon grit or coarse sand over the surface of the compost, then water lightly to settle the compost and plants.

Jade plant (Crassula ovata)

Elephant bush (Portulacaria afra)

Sedum*

*There are more than 200 different types of sedum.

DESERT IN MINIATURE

Succulents like a lot of light, so put the finished mini-desert in a brightly lit window. The plants have a rest period in winter, so water the garden less often then. It is a good idea to put the desert garden outside in a sunny, sheltered spot during the warm summer months, as this helps the plants to grow stronger.

Watering

Water the desert garden only when the surface of the compost has dried out. Desert plants like to dry out and then be well watered.

Trimming

If any of the plants grow "branches" which are long and straggly, cut them off with a small pair of scissors.

SEDUM

ELEPHANT BUSH
(Portulacaria afra)

SEDUM

WART PLANT
(Haworthia attenuata)

FLAMING KATY
This plant's bright flowers last a long time. Replace when it has stopped flowering, as it will not flower again.

The finished garden

The miniature desert garden looks surprisingly green and fresh. To add interest to the garden, you could arrange decorative pebbles or shells around the plants.

JADE PLANT
(Crassula ovata)
This plant is also sometimes known as the money plant.

Replacing plants

HEN AND CHICKENS
(Echeveria)
The name comes from this plant family's habit of growing baby plants around the main plant.

1 If a plant grows too big, gently dig it up with a teaspoon and replant it in a flowerpot or container of its own.

SEDUM SIEBOLDII

2 Replace the big plant with a smaller one. Slide the new plant out of its pot, plant it and firm the soil and sand around it.

STRAWBERRY FEAST

Gardening is not just about growing flowers or indoor plants, you can grow lots of different things to eat too. Try growing your own strawberry plant and watching how the little fruit actually develop. And you do not need masses of space – with a little care, you can grow scrumptious strawberries in a simple flowerpot. Here you can find out what to do and on the next two pages you can see how the flowers and fruit grow.

Young strawberry plant or plants. You can buy these at garden centres from late spring onwards.

You will need

GARDENER'S TOOLS

Trowel

Scissors

Watering can

Loam or soil-based potting compost

A flowerpot for each plant

Gravel or clay pellets

What to do

1 Put a layer of gravel about 1 cm deep in the bottom of the flowerpot, to stop the compost going soggy.

2 Shovel a little potting compost into the flowerpot, leaving plenty of space for the strawberry plant's roots.

Drip tray for each flowerpot

3 If the strawberry plant's roots are all curled up, gently untangle them with your fingers and shake them free of extra soil.

4 Lower the plant into the flowerpot so that its roots touch the potting compost and its crown is just below the pot rim.

5 Fill the flowerpot almost to the top with compost, heaping it up to the base of the plant's leaves. Firm the compost down.

6 Give the plant a good watering. Check the potting compost regularly and water it enough to keep it slightly moist.

27

From Flower To Fruit

Strawberries are woodland fruit and they grow well in the shade, but the fruit will grow and ripen better either indoors or outside, if the plants are kept in a sunny place. Water the compost often enough to keep it slightly moist. Then sit back, wait and watch carefully as the flowers are transformed into perfect, delicious strawberries.

Flowerbud protected by the green, cup-shaped calyx.

The growing plant

1 At first, the plant just grows more and bigger leaves. Then a stem grows and flowerbuds appear at the end of it.

If the plant grows any runners, cut them off at the base. This helps the plant to grow better fruit.

From bud to flower

2 The buds open out into white flowers with yellowish-green centres. When the flower petals die and fall off, the centres of the flowers start to swell.

Swelling centre of flower

Bud

Flower

28

Green strawberry

Flower

Green strawberries

3 The plant is still flowering. The centres of the first flowers now look like small, hard, green strawberries. Keep the plant well-watered while the fruit is forming.

The leaves are still growing

Unripe, green strawberries

Ripe strawberry

The ripening fruit

4 The strawberries grow larger and heavier. As they ripen, they turn a creamy colour, then become tinged with pink. Finally they turn red.

Dying flower

Picking

Pick the strawberries when they are red, keeping the little green caps on.

Pip Planting

Every time you eat fruit, you throw away the pips or stone in the middle, but have you ever thought of planting them instead? If you give the pips the right conditions and are patient, you will be surprised at what will grow: many pips produce handsome plants. The best time of year to plant pips is in the spring. Here you can find out what to do and see how an avocado stone grows.

Grape pips

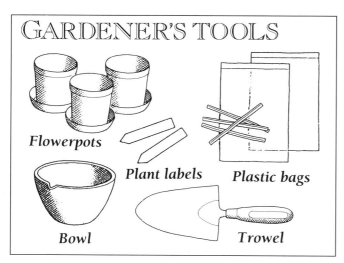

Gardener's Tools

Flowerpots

Plant labels

Plastic bags

Bowl

Trowel

Peach stone

Orange or lemon pips

You will need
Different pips and stones:

Apple pips

Seed and cuttings compost

Avocado stone

What to do

1 Soak big stones in water for 24 hours. Put some compost in a bowl and water it. Stir it well, then fill small pots with the compost.

2 Plant avocado stones pointed end up, sticking out of the compost. Plant pips about 1 cm down in pots of compost.

3 Label each pot to say what is in it. Put each pot in a plastic bag and tie the bag at the top, then put the pots in a warm, dark place.

The growing plant

Check the flowerpots every day. As soon as you see a shoot in one of them, move it to a light place and take off the plastic bag. Water the young plant regularly, just enough to keep the compost moist, and watch it grow. Here you can see the first stages in the development of an avocado plant.

New, young leaves

The first leaves soon grow quite large.

From stone to plant

Avocado stones take six to seven weeks to sprout. The stone splits, a root grows down into the compost and a shoot emerges at the top.

The stem grows quickly and the first leaves begin to open out.

Young side shoots

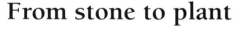

If the plant seems to be growing too tall, pinch out the growing shoot at the top. This encourages the plant to grow bushier.

When the plant shows signs of growing too big for its pot, move it to a fresh pot of compost the next size up.

1

2

3

NEW PLANTS FROM OLD

Take cuttings from your houseplants in the spring and you can grow lots of new plants. A cutting is part of a plant that you cut off and plant so that it grows roots of its own. It may be a leaf, stem or plantlet. Here you can see how to take three types of cutting and over the page you can find out how to care for them.

You will need

Painted leaf begonia
These begonias have striking, coloured heart-shaped leaves and are ideal for leaf cuttings. You can also take leaf cuttings from African violets (Saintpaulias).

Seed and cutting compost

Taking leaf cuttings

Tradescantia
It is easiest to take stem cuttings from tradescantia. Other good plants to take stem cuttings from are geraniums, mint and coleus.

1 Cut a healthy-looking leaf and its stalk off a begonia or African violet. Plant the stalk in a pot of seed and cutting compost.

2 Water the compost to make it moist. Tie a polythene bag over the leaf and flowerpot and put it in a warm place out of the sun.

Taking stem cuttings

Spider plant
These trailing plants grow long runners with baby plantlets at the end, which you can pot up to make new plants.

1 Cut a strong shoot about 6 cm long off the tradescantia or other plant, just below a leaf. Trim the bottom leaves off the stem.

2 Plant the cutting in a pot of seed or potting compost. Or stand it in a glass of water, to watch it grow roots*.

Plantlets

GARDENER'S TOOLS

Water spray

Glass

Trowel

Ties

Scissors

Flowerpots

Watering can

Polythene bags

1 The plantlets at the end of a spider plant's runners have roots. When the roots are 1 cm long, cut plantlets off the runners.

2 Trim the lower leaves off the plantlets, then plant them in small pots of moist compost, making sure the roots are covered.

* Once the cutting has grown roots, you should plant it in compost.

FROM CUTTINGS TO PLANTS

Checking for growth

After a few weeks, take the bags off the pots and tug the cuttings gently. If the cuttings are rooted firmly in the compost, leave the bags off.

Watering

Keep an eye on the cuttings. Water them when the compost has dried out. It is best to put water in the drip trays, not on the compost.

Spraying

Gently spray the cuttings with water from time to time. This cleans the leaves and stems and stops them from drying out.

Here are some young plants growing from different types of cutting. The African violet and begonia started as leaf cuttings.

PAINTED LEAF BEGONIA

SPIDER PLANT
The spider plant was grown from a plantlet. You can pot up plantlets from strawberry geraniums (Saxifraga stolonifera) in the same way.

AFRICAN VIOLET

Encouraging growth

Repotting

If a baby plant is growing too tall and straggly, pick off the growing tips of the shoots. This makes the plant grow bushier.

1 If roots are showing at the bottom of a plant's pot, you should repot the plant. Gently tip the plant out into your hand.

2 Plant it in a new pot, one size larger, filled with fresh new compost. Water the plant and put it in a shady place for about a week.

TRADESCANTIA
This tradescantia cutting has rooted in a glass of water. When the roots are 2-4 cm long, the cutting should be planted in a pot of compost.

AEONIUM
Some succulents grow small plants around their stem. Break these off and plant them in separate pots of compost.

SILVER TREE
This plant was grown from a stem cutting taken in the spring.

35

VEGETABLES IN POTS

You don't need a garden to grow vegetables. You can grow small or dwarf varieties very successfully in flowerpots and other containers on a balcony, strong window ledge, or patio. Here you can see how to plant vegetables. Look at the backs of seed packets to find out when and where to plant them. Turn the page to see some vegetables growing!

GARDENER'S TOOLS

Trowel

Seed trays

Flowerpots

Watering can

Pen (for labels)

Water spray

You will need

Different types of seed:

Potting compost

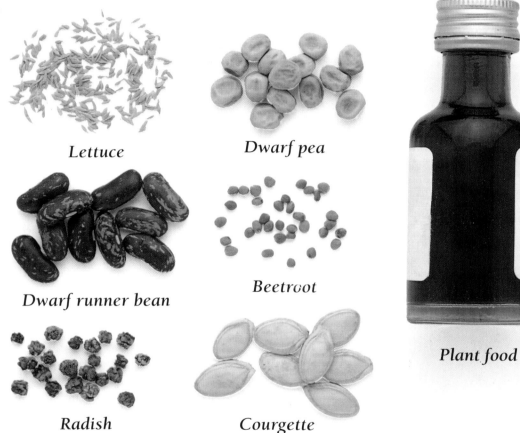

Lettuce

Dwarf pea

Dwarf runner bean

Beetroot

Radish

Courgette

Plant food

What to do

1 Fill the seed trays and flowerpots with compost and water the compost a little, so that it is moist but not soaking wet.

2 Plant big seeds in flowerpots. Push each about 1 cm deep into the compost. Label the pots with the names of the seeds.

3 Plant small seeds in seed trays. Sprinkle them over the compost, then cover them with a thin layer of compost. Label them.

Clay pellets or gravel

Labels

Plastic bags and ties

Garden sticks

4 Spray the seed trays and flowerpots with water. Tie plastic bags over them and put them in a warm, dark place*.

5 As soon as shoots appear, take the plastic bags off the seeds and move them into the light. Spray the compost with water.

6 When the seedlings grow too big for their pots or trays, dig them up very carefully and plant them in separate flowerpots.

* Such as an airing cupboard.

Vegetables Galore

Follow the instructions on the seed packets and remember to water your vegetables often to keep the compost moist. Then watch them grow! Here you can follow the progress of a lettuce and a dwarf green bean plant.

Lettuce

1

Tiny seedlings appear in the seed tray. The first true leaves are beginning to show.

2

One of the small lettuces has been moved to its own pot.

3

Pick the lettuce before its leaves open out too far.

Dwarf Green Bean Plant

1

Remains of seed

First leaves

The stem grows quickly and the plant's first real leaves begin to open out from between the two halves of the old seed.

2

The leaves grow bigger...

3

...and bigger.

5

Young bean forming

Flowers

As the plant grows, twist the stem around a garden stick and tie it in place, to give it support. Spray the flowers with water. This helps the beans to grow.

Tie

Garden stick

HARVESTING
The beans are tastiest when they are small. Pick them when they are about 10 cm long and snap easily when bent.

4

The plant is now growing very fast and young leaves are sprouting everywhere.

WINDOW GARDEN

With a window box you can look out on to a mass of flowers without having to go outside. Choose flowers in one or two colours, or go for a riot of bright colours. Look out for plants with interesting leaves, and for trailing plants to go at the front of the window box. Here you can see what to do. The final result is over the page.

GARDENER'S TOOLS

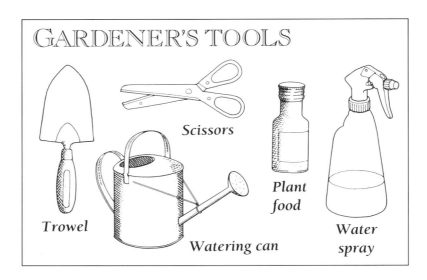

Scissors

Trowel

Watering can

Plant food

Water spray

Busy Lizzy

You will need

Small plants (two or three of each sort)

Marguerite

Soil-based potting compost

Clay pellets, gravel or crocks

A window box with drainage holes in the bottom and a drip tray

Bellflower

Pansy

What to do

1 Fill the bottom of the window box with a layer of clay pellets about 3 cm deep, to stop the compost going soggy.

2 Half fill the window box with potting compost. If the compost is very dry, water it before you start planting anything.

3 Keeping the plants in their pots, arrange where to put them. Tall plants should go at the back and trailing ones at the front.

4 One at a time, take each plant out of its pot and gently loosen its roots by pulling them free from the potting compost.

5 Dig a small hole. Gently put the first plant in, making sure its roots have enough room. Press down the compost round the plant.

6 Plant the other plants. Fill in the gaps between them with compost and press it down firmly, leaving space for watering.

GARDEN IN BLOOM

And here is the finished window box! You can copy this one, or try your own plant arrangements. Ask an adult to help you move the full window box as it is heavy and must sit safely on a strong window ledge. If the window ledge slopes a little, wedge pieces of wood under the front of the box, to keep it level.

Watering

Water the window box enough to keep the compost slightly moist. It will need watering every day in warm weather.

Dead–heading

The plants in the window box will flower for longer if you regularly pick or snip off any dead flower heads.

The finished window box

MARGUERITE

This is a small busy plant that produces pretty daisy-like flowers throughout the summer.

BUSY LIZZY (Impatiens)

Easy to look after, these plants have flat-faced, brightly coloured flowers. They will stay in flower for most of the summer.

Feeding

Once every six weeks or so, "feed" the plants by adding a little liquid plant food to the water in your watering can.

Pest control

The simplest way to get rid of greenfly on the plants is to spray them with warm water with washing-up liquid added to it.

New plants

If one of the plants in the window box dies, carefully dig it up. Plant another plant in its place, pressing the compost firmly around it.

PANSY

We used two apricot-coloured pansies and two purple ones. Keep pansies well-watered and dead-head them often.

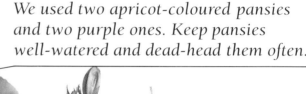

BELLFLOWER (Campanula)

This trailing variety of bellflower can also be grown as an indoor plant. It blooms from late summer to early winter.

HERB FEAST

For centuries people have grown herbs to flavour food, to make medicines and even to keep evil spirits away. Here and on the next three pages you can see how to recreate a traditional ornamental herb garden in a large container, full of useful kitchen herbs.

You will need

Small herb plants:

GARDENER'S TOOLS

Trowel

Watering can

String

Scissors

Pot marjoram

French or flat-leaved parsley
(you need eight small plants)

Lemon thyme

Gravel or clay pellets

Peat or soil-based potting compost

Large, square container

Planting up the container

1 Fill the bottom of the container with a layer of gravel or clay pellets about 3 cm deep. This stops the soil going soggy.

2 Add compost to the container until it is about three quarters full. This allows plenty of space for planting the herbs.

3 Plant the feverfew in the centre of the pot. Plant the parsley in two diagonal lines crossing over the feverfew.

4 Plant the sage, rosemary, marjoram, and thyme in the triangular spaces between the lines of parsley.

5 Press the potting compost down firmly all around the plants. Add more compost if needed. Water the herbs well.

Rosemary

Purple-leaved sage

Feverfew

MINI KNOT GARDEN

Traditional knot gardens were divided into patterns by small hedge plants. In this knot garden, parsley is used to make a simple cross pattern and the other herbs give contrasting colours and textures. Here you can find out more about the herbs used.

PARSLEY

Parsley is one of the most useful kitchen herbs. It likes some shade and a lot of water. It only lasts for one summer, so you will need to replace it if you keep the knot garden for longer.

ROSEMARY

An aromatic, evergreen shrub with small blue flowers in spring. Rosemary grows best in a sunny sheltered place. It grows tall, so keep it well trimmed.

GOLDEN FEVERFEW

A medicinal herb with aromatic golden-green leaves and pretty daisy-like flowers. Prefers a sunny position.

Trimming the herbs

Snip or pick the herbs often, especially the parsley, to help them grow bushy and to keep the shape of the knot garden.

PURPLE SAGE

One of many types of sage. A strongly scented evergreen plant with small, purplish flowers. Likes a sunny place.

LEMON THYME

One of many types of thyme. Dark green leaves with a lemon scent and tiny pink flowers in summer. Likes sun. Much loved by bees and butterflies.

BOUQUET GARNI

This is a small bunch or "bouquet" of fresh herbs used to add flavour to stews and casseroles.

Making a bouquet garni

Cut short sprigs of different herbs and tie them together in a small bunch with a piece of string, as shown.

POT MARJORAM

Strongly flavoured herb with pink or white flowers that attract bees. Likes sun. Perennial that needs to be cut back before winter.

BUSHY TOPS

When you buy vegetables in shops, you think of them as something to eat and may never see what they look like when they are growing in the ground. Vegetables and fruit do not die when they are picked and with a little patience you can grow surprisingly attractive plants from kitchen leftovers. Here you can find out how to grow bushy green plants from carrot and parsnip tops.

Vermiculite or soil-less compost

Carrots

Parsnips

You will need

GARDENER'S TOOLS

Flowerpots

Knife

Water spray

What to do

Fill the flowerpots with vermiculite. Cut off the top of each vegetable. Plant the tops on the vermiculite. Spray with water.

Put the flowerpots in a warm, dark place, such as an airing cupboard. Check them every day to make sure the vermiculite stays moist.

NEW PLANTS

At the first sign of growth, put the flowerpots in a light place. Spray them with water, to keep the vermiculite moist, and they will soon grow into strong, bushy plants. You can move them to larger pots of potting compost as they grow bigger, but they will not grow new carrots or parsnips.